東寺基本情報 Basic Information of the Temple To-ji (Kyo-o-gokoku-ji)

所在地	〒601-8473　京都市南区九条町1
電話	075-691-3325
アクセス	JR京都駅より徒歩約17分、近鉄東寺駅より徒歩約5分。 または、京都市バス東寺南門前、東寺東門前、九条大宮下車すぐ。
公式サイト	日本語：http://www.toji.or.jp/ 英語：http://www.toji.or.jp/en/index.html

Address	Kujo-cho 1, Minami-ku, Kyoto 601-8473, Japan
Phone	075-691-3325
Access	About 17 minutes' walk from JR Kyoto station; about 5 minutes' walk from Kintetsu Toji station; close to each of the Kyoto City bus stops (Toji Minamimon-mae, Toji Higashimon-mae, and Kujo-Omiya)
Official websites	Japanese: http://www.toji.or.jp/ English: http://www.toji.or.jp/en/index.html

金堂・講堂拝観時間	午前8:00 〜午後5:00
Kondo and Kodo open	8:00 A.M.–5:00 P.M.

五重塔初層公開　　　　　　　　　　　　宝物館特別公開
Five-story Pagoda (first level) open to the public　　　Treasury Museum open to the public

1月1日〜5日　　　　　　　　　　　　春期：3月20日〜5月25日
January 1–5　　　　　　　　　　　　　秋期：9月20日〜11月25日
　　　　　　　　　　　　　　　　　　　March 20–May 25 and September 20–November 25

［目次］ / Contents

東寺基本情報	3	Basic Information of the Temple To-ji
年中行事	4	Annual Ceremonies and Festivals
東寺の歴史	5	Major Events in the History of the Temple To-ji
東寺はどんなお寺か	6	About the Temple To-ji
御堂と御本尊	10	Principal Buildings and Their Main Images
歴史背景　1	18	Historical Background 1
歴史背景　2	20	Historical Background 2
名宝と文化財	22	Treasures and Cultural Properties
歴史的資料『東宝記』	32	*Tobo-ki*: Exceptional Historical Material
「大日如来」写仏	35	Drawing the Buddha Dainichi Nyorai

［表紙写真］
講堂の軍荼利明王立像（左）と不動明王坐像（右）

Cover photo
Standing statue of the Wisdom King Gundari (*left*) and seated statue of the Wisdom King Fudo Myo-ō (*right*) housed in the Kodo (Lecture Hall)

年中行事 *Annual Ceremonies and Festivals*

The year-end Kobo Market on 21th December

To-ji Temple
Shogakukan archives

This book is an English edition of TOJI, KOJI WO MEGURU #3 published by SHOGAKUKAN in 2007 with extensive additions and modifications.

All photographs ©2016 To-ji

English translation and redesign ©Interbooks

Published by
SHOGAKUKAN
2-3-1 Hitotsubashi Chiyoda-ku,
Tokyo 101-8001 JAPAN

http://www.shogakukan.co.jp

All rights reserved.
No part of this publication may be reproduced in any form or by any means, graphic, electronic or mechanical, including photocopying and recording by an information storage and retrieval system, without written permission from the publisher.

To-ji Temple, Shogakukan archives
© 2016 SHOGAKUKAN
Printed in Japan
ISBN978-4-09-105443-2

January	1–5	New Year Celebration
	3	New Year Service (at the Miedo)
	8-14	Seven-day New Year Ceremonies for the Protection of the Nation (at the Kanjo-in)
	21	New Year Kobo Market (in the temple compound)
	28	New Year Service (at the Kodo)
March	15	*Goma* Prayer Services for Peace for Humanity and Global Security (at the Chinju Hachiman Shrine)
	21	Spring Equinoctial Services
April	21	Annual Ceremonies to Commemorate Kobo Daishi's Death (at the Miedo); exposition of *ema* plaques (at the Kanjo-in Akai well)
June	15	Ceremonies to Commemorate Kobo Daishi's Birth (at the Miedo)
August	15	Buddhist Lantern Festival (at the Dainichido)
September	21	Autumn Equinoctial Services
November	15	Chinju Hachiman Bosatsu Services (at the Chinju Hachiman Shrine)
December	21	Year-end Kobo Market (in the temple compound)

* * * *

First day of each month	Ceremonies Dedicated to the Great Wisdom Sutra (at the Miedo)
15th day of each month	Fusatsu Ceremonies for Intensified Meditation (at the Miedo)
21st day of each month	Monthly Ceremonies to Commemorate Kobo Daishi's Death (at the Miedo)
First Sunday of each month	Antiques Market (in the vicinity of Great South Gate)

東寺の歴史

Major Events in the History of the Temple To-ji

796 C.E.	Initiation of the construction of the paired To-ji (East Temple) and Sai-ji (West Temple) in the capital city, then known as Heian-kyo (present-day Kyoto).
823	The Emperor Saga (786–842) put the great Buddhist priest and scholar Kukai (774–835) in charge of To-ji while it was being built as a state-sponsored temple and the fundamental training center for the Shingon School of Buddhism.
824	When Kukai was appointed construction administrator, building of the To-ji compound began in earnest.
835	Kukai entered eternal Samadhi (meditative consciousness) on Mount Koya.
839	The ensemble of statues for the Kodo (Lecture Hall) was finished, completing a multidimensional mandala or symbolic representation of the universe. *Kaigen* (eye-opening) ceremonies were held to consecrate it.
843	First Denpo Kanjo (Esoteric Buddhist Dharma-transmission Ceremonies) were performed at the Kanjo-in sub-temple.
883	The To-ji Five-story Pagoda was completed at about this time.
1055	Lightning struck the Five-story Pagoda, which burned completely. Owing to financial difficulties, the temple compound fell into disrepair.
1197	Repairs on the buildings and statuary by the priest Mongaku (1139–1203) under the direction of the Kamakura shogun Minamoto Yoritomo (1147–99) neared completion.
1308	The cloistered Emperor Go-Uda (1267–1324) prayed for the prosperity of To-ji before a statue of Kobo Daishi Kukai and donated numerous estates to the temple.
1336	By setting up a stronghold on its grounds, the Muromachi shogun Ashikaga Takauji (1305–58) made To-ji a scene for the disturbances of the so-called period of the Northern and Southern Courts (1336–92).
1352	The priest-scholar Goho (1306–62) compiled the eight-volume *Tobo-ki*, a history and general account of To-ji.
1486	Various buildings and part of the Kodo (Lecture Hall) destroyed by fire during peasant uprisings.
1497	Reconstruction of the Kodo (Lecture Hall) at about this time.
1568	The powerful warlord Oda Nobunaga (1534–82) established a stronghold at To-ji, thus avoiding a temple-capture campaign.
1594	The Five-story Pagoda rebuilt by the warlord and nation unifier Toyotomi Hideyoshi (1536–98).
1603	The Kondo (Golden Hall), the temple's main hall, rebuilt by Toyotomi Hideyori (1593–1615), the third son of Toyotomi Hideyoshi.
1644	The Five-story Pagoda, which had been destroyed by fire in 1635, rebuilt by Edo shogun Tokugawa Iemitsu (1604–51).
1871	Discontinuance of the traditional Seven-day New Year Ceremonies for the Protection of the Nation was a great blow to both To-ji and the Shingon School of Buddhism in general (the ceremonies were reinstated in 1883).
1930	A statue of the Thousand-arm Kannon Bodhisattva seriously damaged and statues of the Four Heavenly Kings burned in a fire that destroyed the Jikido (Temple Refectory).
1965	The To-ji Treasury Museum opened to the general public.
1994	The temple registered as a UNESCO World Heritage Site as one of 17 Historic Monuments of Ancient Kyoto.
1995	Ceremonies held to commemorate the 1,200th anniversary of the temple's founding.
2000	Completion of repairs (started in 1997) of the statues in the Kodo (Lecture Hall).

東寺はどんなお寺か

About the Temple To-ji

The Center of Shingon Esoteric-Buddhist Learning and Training

Nighttime illumination of the To-ji Five-story Pagoda in spring
For more than 370 years, the To-ji Five-story Pagoda, as restored by the Edo shogun Tokugawa Iemitsu (1604–51), has been one of the most enduring symbols of the city of Kyoto. With a height of about 55 meters, it is the tallest old pagoda in Japan. The Nandaimon (Great South Gate) in the wall to the right of the pagoda in this photograph burned down in 1868. The present gate was formerly the west gate of the temple Rengeo-in. It was given to To-ji in 1895 to commemorate the 1,100th anniversary of the temple's founding.

● Symbol of Kyoto

Though many people may not realize that To-ji is the head temple of the To-ji Shingon Buddhism, everyone recognizes its Five-story Pagoda (Japanese National Treasure). The very sight of the pagoda on television or its mention by tourist guides immediately calls the city of Kyoto to mind. The temple is also a virtual monument to the fervor **Kukai (774–835, also known by the posthumous title Kobo Daishi)** devoted to spreading Shingon Esoteric-Buddhist teachings.

As great a religious genius as Kukai was, he did not live to see the completion of the temple pagoda. It has burned down on several occasions; and the building as it now stands is the fifth reconstruction, erected during the period of the third Edo shogun Tokugawa Iemitsu (1604–51). Today's Kondo (Golden Hall), the temple's main hall, is a reconstruction from the time of Toyotomi Hideyori (1593–1615), a son of the famous warlord Toyotomi Hideyoshi (1536–98). Oddly, the Toyotomi family revered Kobo Daishi at a time when Tokugawa authority was on the rise; the fortunes of the Toyotomi clan were declining; and Osaka Castle, which they built, fell.

● Kukai Set Some Conditions

Though geniuses like him are said to live in isolation, Kukai enjoyed the important support of the Emperor Saga (786–842), who shared his

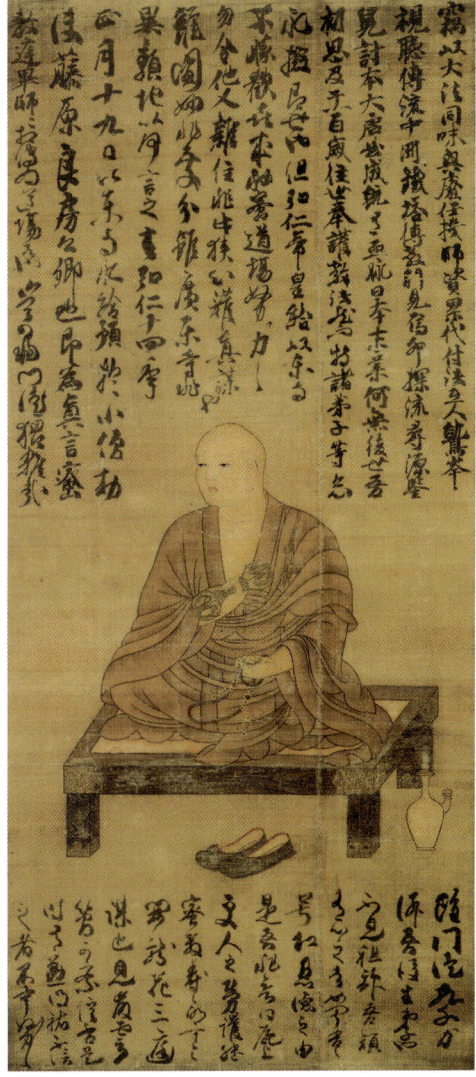

Painting of Kobo Daishi (*Dangi Honzon*)
Silk; vertical dimension 141.9 cm, horizontal dimension 61.7 cm; Kamakura period (1184–1333); Japanese Important Cultural Property; possession of the To-ji
This painting is displayed in the Miedo (Kukai Residence Hall) as a primary object of reverence when sermons or discussions of Buddhist teachings *(dangi)* are held. It was presented to the temple in 1313. The top and bottom laudatory texts are said to have been written by the cloistered Emperor Go-Uda (1267–1324), who deeply honored Kobo Daishi. The general content consists of Kobo Daishi's *Nijugokajo Goyuigo* (25-article will), forbidding coexistence with other Buddhist schools.

cultivation and tastes. When Saga expressed the wish to put him in charge of To-ji, Kukai accepted but with firmly stated conditions: "I want to make To-ji a fundamental training center for Shingon Esoteric Buddhism. And so, I would like you to forbid coexistence at To-ji with other Buddhist schools."

His request broke with common sense among the so-called Six Schools of Nara—Kegon, Hosso, and so on—in which priests studying in any area could attain to the highest ranks. Nonetheless, the Emperor Saga agreed to Kukai's ardent insistence on making To-ji a temple for Shingon Buddhism exclusively.

In 794, in a mere ten years, the Emperor Kanmu (737–806) had the capital of Japan moved from Nagaoka-kyo (southwest of Kyoto) to Heian-kyo (present-day Kyoto). An avenue called Suzaku Oji running north and south divided the city plan into east and west blocks. Flanking it on the south edge of the city, two temples protecting the state were erected. The one on the east is To-ji (East Temple); the one on the west was Sai-ji (West Temple), which has not survived.

The building of the temples was no easy matter. Owing to the need to pacify indigenous peoples in the north of the country and with repeated relocation of the capital, they remained unfinished under the Emperor Kanmu and his successor Heizei (774–824). By the time when the Emperor Saga put Kukai in charge of To-ji, only the Kondo and small priest quarters had been completed.

Aerial view of the To-ji compound
To-ji is situated at what might be called the entrance to the city of Kyoto. On a straight line running from the Nandaimon (Great South Gate, foreground) to the Hokudaimon (Great North Gate) are the Kondo (Golden Hall), the Kodo (Lecture Hall), and the Jikido (Temple Refectory). In the foreground to the right of the north-south axis is the Five-story Pagoda; on the left is the Kanjo-in sub-temple (ordinarily closed to the public). In the rear ground are the sub-temples Kanchi-in, Hobodai-in, and the Shingon School's Rakunan High School and its affiliated junior high school.

● Mandala in Sculpture Form

No buildings from Kukai's time survive in the To-ji compound of today. But a group of statues, many of which are Japanese National Treasures, housed in the Kodo (Lecture Hall) remains to transmit his philosophy.

A mandala is a plane pictorial representation of Buddhist teachings on the basis of scriptures like the Kongocho-gyo (Vajarasekhara Sutra) and the Ninno-gyo (The Humane King Sutra). Its central feature, and the central being in Shingon Esoteric Buddhism, is the primordial Buddha known as Dainichi Nyorai (Vairocana), the source from which all other Buddhas and bodhisattvas arise. Kukai said that Shingon Esoteric Buddhism cannot be conveyed vocally. The mandala is an expedient for conveying its meaning in a nonverbal way. To make it still easier to understand, Kukai devised a multidimensional version involving 21 appropriately positioned statues of important Buddhist beings. Perhaps its meaning becomes clearer if this multidimensional representation is thought of as a kind of pop-up picture book manifesting Kukai's philosophy. The power emanating from each of these statues usually leaves first-time visitors to To-ji Kodo speechless.

Shingon Esoteric Buddhism teaches the doctrine known in Japanese as *Sokushin Jobutsu*, or attaining Buddhahood in the present body by maintaining bodily health, being moderate in speech, and purifying the mind. The attainment takes place in the here and now without repeated cycles of birth, death, and rebirth. Kobo Daishi Kukai taught that all human beings possess the Buddha seed. They can see the Buddha if their minds are pure but they cannot if their minds are impure.

● Kukai's Concept of the To-ji Compound

The building known as the Miedo is the center of fervent reverence for

Standing statue of Jikokuten, Heavenly King of the East

Wood; figure height 183.0 cm; Heian period (794–1185); Japanese National Treasure; housed in the Kodo

One of the four Heavenly Kings of the cardinal directions, Jikokuten protects the east. This powerful statue is the first thing a visitor sees upon entering the building. He holds a treasure sword in one hand and tramples on a demon. Carved of a single block of wood, the figure bears traces of its original coloration.

Commemoration of Kobo Daishi at the Miedo

Ceremonies commemorating Kobo Daishi are held on April 21, a very special day as the anniversary of his death. On this occasion, the gate of the normally closed Kanjo-in sub-temple is opened, revealing the votary *ema* plaques hanging by the Akai well.

Kobo Daishi Kukai himself. In a gentle, traditional Japanese style, it has a hip-and-gable roof covered with cypress-bark shingles. The site is said to have been the location of quarters for Kukai himself. He considered the overall temple compound to be a reproduction of the mandala symbolic representation of the Buddhist cosmos. After Kukai's death, the Miedo became sacred ground.

Kobo Daishi Kukai was unable to achieve two of his most cherished goals: the erection of the Five-story Pagoda and the construction of the Kanjo-in sub-temple. The 80 fragmentary relics, said to be those of the historic Buddha Shakyamuni, that he received in Tang-dynasty (618–907) China and brought back with him were to have been placed in the stone foundation beneath the pagoda central pillar. In 835, the year in which he entered eternal Samadhi (meditative consciousness), Seven-day New Year Ceremonies for the Protection of the Nation were held at the Shingon-in in the imperial palace. Kobo Daishi Kukai had ardently hoped they would take place at To-ji. Today, held at the To-ji Kanjo-in, these ceremonies, consisting of prayers for the protection of the state, the prosperity of the imperial family, and abundant crops, are the most prestigious of all Shingon Esoteric-Buddhist services. Ordinarily, the Kanjo-in is closed to the public. Now designated UNESCO World Heritage Site, To-ji is changing with the times.

A To-ji pilgrims' song says that Kobo Daishi Kukai vowed that, though his body was on Mount Koya (another center of Shingon Buddhism in Wakayama Prefecture), his heart would be at To-ji. When, departing for Mount Koya, he passed through the To-ji Rengemon gate in the northwestern part of the compound. It is said that the Wisdom King Fudo Myo-ō shed tears at his departure and that lotus flowers bloomed in his footsteps.

御堂と御本尊
Principal Buildings and Their Main Images

Kobo Daishi Kukai said that the inner teachings of Shingon Esoteric Buddhism cannot be conveyed with plane representations. Although an ordinary mandala is a plane picture, out of his kindly desire to convey the essence of Esoteric Buddhism, Kobo Daishi Kukai decided to make a multidimensional mandala employing suitably arranged Buddhist statues in the Kodo.

Although a main image is a principal object of reverence, for many years the statues at To-ji were strictly concealed. Nevertheless, faith in Kobo Daishi never waned. A reason for this phenomenon relates to a belief in close association with Kobo Daishi himself. Bearing staves and dressed in white, pilgrims wear woven hats bearing the words *Dogyo Ninin*, meaning when you go together (with Kobo Daishi), you are never alone. He is always with you.

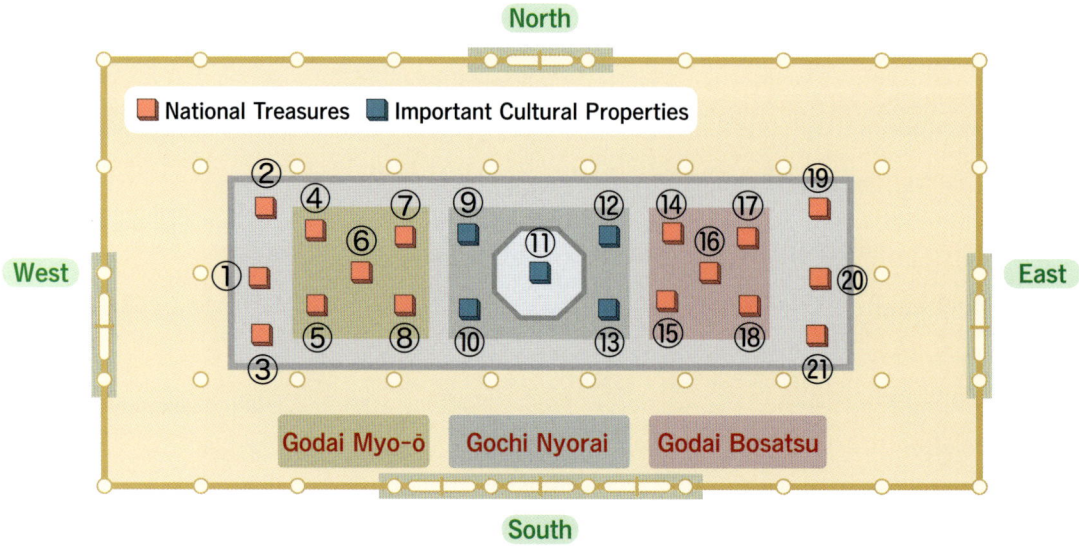

Placements of statues in the Kodo (Lecture Hall)

① Deva Taishakuten
② Heavenly King of the West Komokuten
③ Heavenly King of the South Zochoten
④ Wisdom King Daiitoku
⑤ Wisdom King Gundari
⑥ Wisdom King Fudo Myo-ō
⑦ Wisdom King Kongo Yasha
⑧ Wisdom King Gozanze
⑨ Dhyani Buddha Fukujoju
⑩ Dhyani Buddha Amida
⑪ Buddha Dainichi Nyorai (Vairocana)
⑫ Dhyani Buddha Ashuku
⑬ Dhyani Buddha Hosho
⑭ Great Bodhisattva Kongogo
⑮ Great Bodhisattva Kongoho
⑯ Great Bodhisattva Kongo Haramitta
⑰ Great Bodhisattva Kongosatta
⑱ Great Bodhisattva Kongoho
⑲ Heavenly King of the North Tamonten
⑳ Deva Bonten
㉑ Heavenly King of the East Jikokuten

Kodo (Lecture Hall)

The Kodo is part of Kobo Daishi's plan to make To-ji the main training and learning temple for Shingon Esoteric Buddhism. In keeping with his ideas, a large number of Buddhist statues are arranged in the hall (see left page). The central element is a seated statue of the Buddha Dainichi Nyorai (Vairocana), who is in turn central to a surrounding group of Five Dhyani Buddhas (according to the Diamond-world Mandala, beings who have attained the ultimate stage of enlightenment).

Seated statue of the Buddha Dainichi Nyorai (Vairocana)
Wood; figure height 280.0 cm; Muromachi period (1336–1573); Japanese Important Cultural Property

Unlike most statues of Buddhas, Dainichi Nyorai wears a crown and rich necklace and bracelets. The right palm is wrapped around the left index finger in what is called the knowledge-fist mudra (*chiken-in*). Likened to the sun, Dainichi Nyorai illuminates all things with the light of mercy and wisdom.

Kodo
Muromachi period; Japanese Important Cultural Property
Immediately adjacent to the Kondo, the Kodo burned in 1486 and was rebuilt in 1491. Its hip-and-gable roof is covered with traditional Japanese tiles. The building rests on original foundations and cornerstones.

Statues in the Kodo

Five Dhyani Buddhas (Japanese Important Cultural Properties); Five Great Bodhisattvas (Japanese National Treasures); Four Heavenly Kings of the Cardinal Directions (Japanese National Treasures); Five Wisdom Kings (Japanese National Treasures); Brahma Deva and Indra Deva (Japanese National Treasure). All of them are wooden and date entirely from the Heian period (794–1185), except the Five Dhyani Buddhas and the central of the Five Great Bodhisattvas, which were mended in the middle ages.

This view is westward from the east side of the interior. The Buddha Dainichi Nyorai (Vairocana), left of center in the photograph, wearing a crown and with the highest aureole, is the monarch of Shingon Esoteric teachings. The statues fill the interior space without clutter or excess. If represented in plane form, their layout would produce a mandala picture.

Kondo (Golden Hall)

The Kondo, the temple's main hall, was the only building completed in the compound when the Emperor Saga put Kobo Daishi Kukai in charge of To-ji. The original building burned down during the Bunmei peasant uprising of 1486. The Kondo as it stands today is a reconstruction made with the support of Toyotomi Hideyori, the third son of Toyotomi Hideyoshi. The main image, a triad consisting of the Healing Buddha Yakushi Nyorai and his attendant bodhisattvas Nikko and Gakko, is a masterwork by the Buddhist sculptor Kosei.

The calmer Kondo gives visitors who have just been overwhelmed by the mighty statues in the Kodo a chance to catch their breath. This does not, however, impair the impact made by the Yakushi Nyorai triad, which becomes more impressive the longer one looks at it.

Standing statue of the Bodhisattva Nikko
Wood; figure height 270.0 cm; Momoyama period (1573–1600); Japanese Important Cultural Property

The only sculpture in the Kondo is a triad consisting of the Healing Buddha Yakushi Nyorai and two attendant bodhisattvas, Nikko (Sunlight) and Gakko (Moonlight). Standing on the right (Nikko) and left (Gakko) of Yakushi Nyorai, they generate a cool, reserved atmosphere. All three statues in the triad were made in 1603.

Kondo
Momoyama period (1573–1600); Japanese National Treasure

The imposing and stately Kondo is a reconstruction of 1603. Ceremonies commemorating its completion were held in 1606. It is the largest building at To-ji. Though it has a double roof, inside it is a single story with a ceiling height of 12 meters. In the center of the façade, the eaves roof is elevated to accommodate a small, two-leaf window. The hall is a masterpiece of Momoyama-period large-hall architecture.

Seated statue of the Healing Buddha Yakushi Nyorai
Wood; figure height 290.0 cm; Momoyama period; Japanese Important Cultural Property
Yakushi Nyorai is believed to heal the illnesses of the ordinary people and guard against evil spirits. Seven small figures of Yakushi Nyorai are set into the aureole behind the main figure. Around the pedestal stand individualized figures of the Twelve Divine Generals, the guardian deities who accompany Yakushi Nyorai.

Seated statue of Kobo Daishi
Wood; figure height 83.3 cm; Kamakura period (1185–1333); Japanese National Treasure
The oldest portrait sculpture of Kobo Daishi, the statue was produced by the sculptor Kosho, a son of the master sculptor Unkei, in 1233. In this year the temple Sai-ji disappeared from history with the burning of its Five-story Pagoda. The statue was designated a Japanese National Treasure in 2000.

Miedo (Kukai Residence Hall)

Located in the northwest of the compound, the Miedo is a center for worship of Kobo Daishi himself. Services devoted to his image started in 1233, when a statue of Kobo Daishi was installed. The building burned in 1379 but was immediately rebuilt. In the Japanese style, it has a gently sloping roof covered with cypress-bark shingles. Kobo Daishi's residence was once located on the site where the Miedo now stands. In addition to the statue of Kobo Daishi, it houses a statue of the Wisdom King Fudo Myo-ō that is usually not on public view.

Miedo
Namboku-cho period (period of the Northern and Southern Courts, 1336–92); Japanese National Treasure
This compound building is divided into a front and a rear hall. It is always open to the public. On the 21st of each month, a day for commemorating Kobo Daishi, visitors touring the temple can be seen stopping at the Miedo for a rest. It is the only building at To-ji where people can remove their footwear, enter, and sit.

Five-story Pagoda

A symbol of the To-ji, the Five-story Pagoda was completed over 50 years after Kobo Daishi's death. Although he requested its construction in 826, apparently it was not actually completed until 883. It has burned down on several occasions; and the present building is its fifth reconstruction, completed in 1644 on contributions from the third Edo shogun Tokugawa Iemitsu. With a height of about 55 meters, it is the tallest wooden pagoda in Japan.

First-level interior of the Five-story Pagoda
Richly colored paintings of the Eight Shingon Founders; seated statues of the Four Dhyani Buddhas, including Amida; and various bodhisattvas are housed on the pagoda first level. There is no statue of the main object of reverence, Buddha Dainichi Nyorai (Vairocana), thought to be represented by the square-section central pillar. It is said that one of the 80 relics of the historic Buddha Shakyamuni that Kobo Daishi brought back from Tang-dynasty (618–907) China were placed in the foundation under this pillar. The first level of the pagoda is open from the first to the fifth of January of each year.

Five-story Pagoda
Edo period (1603–1868); Japanese National Treasure
With a feeling of stability and a largely unornamented exterior, this fifth reconstruction of the Five-story Pagoda inspires in the person observing it from below a sense of the building in its original form. The fourth reconstruction burned down in 1635. Construction on the building as it is today started in 1641. It was completed and ready to have Buddhist sculpture enshrined in 1644.

歴史背景　*Historical Background*

Two Temples—To-ji and Sai-ji— and Their Contrasting Fates

Reconstructed model of the capital city Heian-kyo (present-day Kyoto)
The city of Heian-kyo was planned on a checker-board scheme with two temples—To-ji (East Temple) and Sai-ji (West Temple)—symmetrically placed on the south boundary on either side of the main thoroughfare. The Kyoto city government prepared this model (scale: 1/1,000), which is on display at the Kyoto City Heiankyo Sousei-kan Museum.

A New Capital: Heian-kyo

In ancient Japan, the location of the capital city changed periodically. In 794 the Emperor Kanmu (737–806) abandoned the city of Nagaoka (southwest of Kyoto) less than ten years after its foundation and created a new capital called Heian-kyo. Nagaoka-kyo had come to be regarded as unpropitious for several reasons. Fujiwara Tanetsugu (737–85), minister in charge of construction at that time, was assassinated. Crown Prince Sawara (750?–85), Kanmu's younger brother, was suspected of complicity in the crime and exiled to Awaji Island but starved himself to death on the way there.

At Heian-kyo, at the southern end of the thoroughfare called Suzaku Oji (present-day Senbon-dori) was positioned a gate called Rajomon. On either side of the gate two national guardian temples, To-ji (East Temple) on the east and Sai-ji (West Temple) on the west, were built. In the hope of preventing the emergence of the kind of power exerted by vast religious institutions in and around Nara, these were the only two temples permitted in the new capital city. But, owing to huge financial drains caused by efforts to suppress non-Yamato tribes in the north of the country, funds for the two were not always available.

The throne passed from Kanmu (737–806) to Heizei (774–824) and then to Saga (786–842), who put the great priest and scholar Kukai (774–835) in charge of To-ji in 823. Although 30 years had passed since the capital was transferred to Heian-kyo, when Kukai took charge of To-ji, the only completed building in the compound was the radiant Kondo (Golden Hall). All the rest was weed-clogged vacant land.

It is worth noting that, at a time when humble housing for other Buddhist sects was forbidden, thanks to Kukai's persistence, the imperial court promised provisions for 50 priests at To-ji. The number was ultimately reduced to 25, probably because of the court's financial problems. In his later years, Kukai, who entered eternal Samadhi (meditative consciousness) at the age of 62, devoted his energies to buildings at To-ji and at the Shingon monastery at Mount Koya in Wakayama Prefecture.

The distinctive multidimensional mandala, or symbolic representation of the Esoteric-Buddhist world, composed of a group of striking statues in the Kodo (Lecture Hall) was more or less complete before Kukai's entry into eternal Samadhi. The much longed-for Kanjo-in sub-temple was built after this event. And the five-story pagoda, an absolutely essential symbol of an official temple, was not finished until 883, 50 years after Kukai entered eternal Samadhi. The compound did not reach its full grandeur until 80 years after the transfer of the capital to Heian-kyo.

Site of the Rajomon gate

A stone monument standing in a small park bears an inscription indicating where the gate called Rajomon once stood. Surrounded by children's play equipment, the monument faces Kujo-dori street. The city-bus stop Rajomon preserves the gate's name.

Memorial marker and corner stone at the Sai-ji site

A walk from To-ji Rengemon gate leads to a park where Sai-ji once stood. The Kyoto City Karahashi Primary School occupies the old temple site. Excavations begun in 1959 have ascertained the locations of such buildings as the Kondo (Golden Hall). The Sai-ji site is a registered Japanese National Historic Site.

Downfall of Sai-ji

The fates of To-ji and Sai-ji differed radically. Sai-ji was situated symmetrically with To-ji on the western side of the great Rajomon gate on the southern boundary of the city. On the same scale as its eastern counterpart, it was entrusted to the monk Shubin (dates of birth and death unknown), who had studied Hosso and Sanron Buddhism in Nara and was thoroughly well versed in Shingon Esoteric Buddhism as well. At the time of their foundings, Sai-ji was ranked somewhat above To-ji. Its five-story pagoda was not built until the tenth century, or considerably later than that of To-ji.

The Sai-ji, which remained a state-sponsored temple, suffered a great fire in 990 and burned down completely in 1136. It seems that aristocrats in the Heian period (794–1185) regarded it as virtually a total ruin. When the five-story pagoda, the sole surviving building, burned in 1233, the temple was completely destroyed. No voices were raised in favor of its reconstruction.

In contrast, the To-ji remained very much alive as the fundamental training temple for Shingon Esoteric Buddhism. Behind its continued vitality were efforts devoted to restoring the compound by the monk known as the Venerable Mongaku (1139–1203) of the temple Kyoto Takaosan-ji (Jingo-ji). Senyo Mon'in (1181–1252), Imperial Princess and daughter of the cloistered Emperor Go-Shirakawa (1127–1192), donated estates to the temple and a miniature five-story pagoda (height 1.6 meters, Japanese Important Cultural Property), which is now housed in the To-ji Treasury Museum. Factors of this kind enabled To-ji to make a fresh start as a temple devoted to faith in Kobo Daishi.

But the prosperity was impermanent because it depended greatly on the influence of people in authority. Holder of vast manorial estates, To-ji lost much of its fame with the shift from an aristocratic to a warrior-dominated society. Hard times arrived again in the late 19th century, when the Tokugawa shogunate came to an end. Certainly very important in the continued prosperity of the temple has been the amazing attractive force of nameless individuals with deep-rooted faith in Kobo Daishi Kukai. Perhaps also of great significance is the mysterious appeal of this great monk and scholar, generally considered to have been a very charismatic human being.

The great Rajomon gate, which was flanked by the two temples, was the entrance to Heian-kyo. The late-Heian-period collection of tales called the *Konjaku Monogatarishu* (Anthology of tales of the past) describes the gate as in ruins, which is certainly its state in the short story "Rashomon" by the Japanese author Akutagawa Ryunosuke (1892–1927). The statue of Tobatsu Bishamonten (see page 29) now in the To-ji Treasury Museum is said once to have been housed in the upper story of the Rajomon gate.

Historical Background

Kukai, a Great Buddhist Course-setter

Over the Seas to Tang-dynasty China, from the *Kobo Daishi Gyojo E-kotoba* picture scrolls, Vol. 3
Paper; width 34 cm, length 2,019 cm (Vol. 3); Namboku-cho period (1336–92); Japanese Important Cultural Property; possession of the To-ji
This scroll depiction of the biography of Kobo Daishi Kukai was produced in the period of the Northern and Southern Courts. This segment shows the boat carrying Kobo Daishi encountering a storm at sea. Owing to the poor navigational skills of the time, the trip to Tang-dynasty was so mortally perilous that more than half of the official-embassy vessels undertaking are said to have sunk. Kukai's boat reached the capital Chang'an but only after extended periods of drifting. Originating in India, the teachings of Esoteric Buddhism were translated into Chinese and introduced into Chang'an, which became a prime center for their study.

Gilded-bronze Reliquary
Cast bronze; height 49.5 cm; Heian period (794-1185); Japanese Important Cultural Property; possession of the To-ji

The To-ji possesses relics of the historic Buddha Shakyamuni brought by Kukai from Tang-dynasty China. This reliquary is thought to have been used in Seven-day New Year Ceremonies for the Protection of the Nation.

China and Back

Paying his own way, in 804, at the age of 31, Kukai (774–835, also known by the posthumous title Kobo Daishi) traveled to Tang-dynasty (618–907) China to study. With him was another great priest Saicho (767–822), posthumously awarded the title Dengyo Daishi. Kukai went to the temple Qinglong-zi, where he studied the secret teachings of Shingon (Zhenyan in Chinese) Esoteric Buddhism under the priest Huiguo (746–805) and received the religious name Henjo Kongo. In 806, he returned to Japan by way of Mingzhou. Though in China for only two years, he managed to study numerous subjects including civil engineering and pharmacy.

Upon his return, he submitted to Takashina Tonari (757–818), the official in charge of the mission to Tang-dynasty, the *Goshorai Mokuroku*, a catalogue of the many mandalas, esoteric texts, and ritual appurtenances he brought back with him. But for some reason he was denied permission to enter the capital. At first, he spent some time at the temple Kanzeon-ji, in Dazaifu (an ancient city in Fukuoka Prefecture). The following year, he moved to Izumi (the southern part of Osaka Prefecture). He was finally allowed to enter the capital three years later, during the reign of the Emperor Saga (786–842).

He moved to the temple Takaosan-ji (Jingo-ji; Kyoto Prefecture), where he did astonishing work. He conferred the initiation of the Mandala of the Two Worlds—the Diamond-world Mandala and the Womb-world Mandala—on Saicho, the founder of Japanese Tendai Buddhism. For a while he remained at the Otokuni-dera temple (Kyoto Prefecture) then returned to Takaosan-ji.

In 816, at the age of 43, he began work at Mount Koya in Kishu (present-day Wakayama Prefecture). Receiving official sanction from the Emperor Saga, with whom he was on close terms, he took the first steps in creating a vast monastery compound and chose this sacred place as the lo-

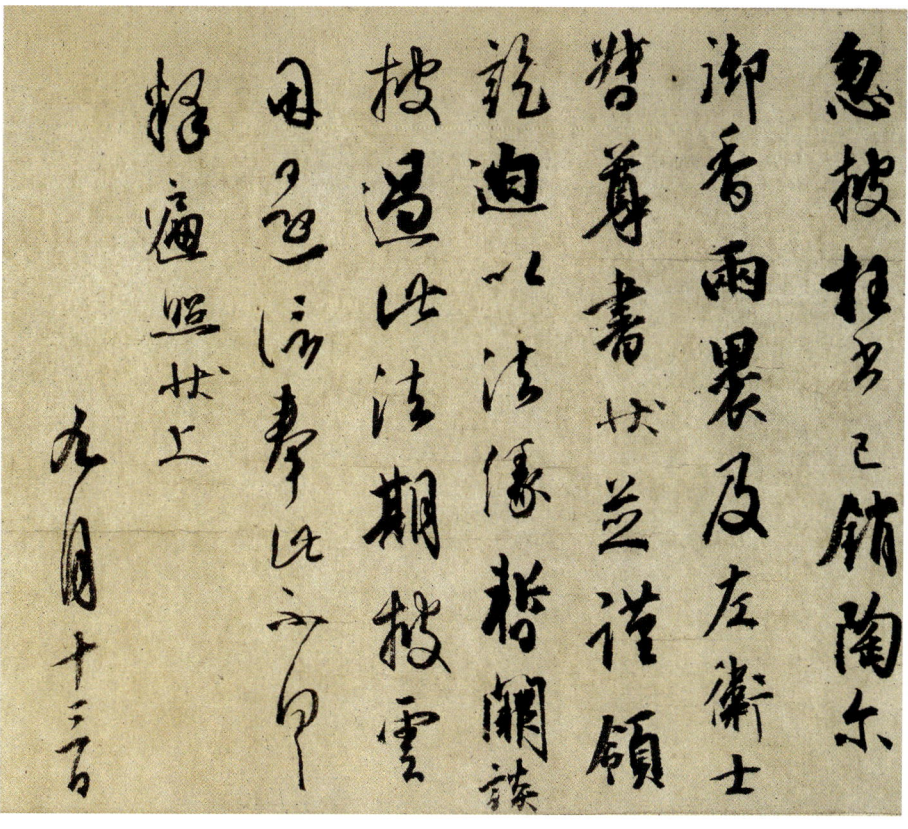

Fushinjo Epistolary Scroll (second letter of the _Sekitoku Santsu_ three letters)
Width 28.8 cm, length 157.9 cm; Heian period (794–1185); Japanese National Treasure; possession of the To-ji

This set of letters sent by Kukai to the great priest and scholar Saicho has been arranged in scroll form. Because the first letter starts with characters *fu* and *shin*, the scroll is named *Fushinjo*. The second letter deals with such things as thanks for some incense presented by Saicho. Together with the Emperor Saga and Tachibana Hayanari (782?–844), Kukai ranks as one of the three outstanding calligraphers referred to as the Sanpitsu. This example reveals his free and fluid calligraphic style.

cation for his own entry into eternal Samadhi.

In 823 he was put in charge of To-ji. Developed simultaneously with the building of the capital Heian-kyo, this temple was to be dedicated to prayers for the spiritual protection of the state. When Kukai took charge of it, however, there was nothing on the grounds but the Kondo, the temple's main hall, and some small priests' quarters.

Kukai devoted all his efforts to making To-ji a fundamental training center for Shingon Esoteric Buddhism up until 835, when he entered eternal Samadhi (meditative consciousness) at Mount Koya. One element in this project was the building of Kodo (lecture hall) based on his own ideas. It is said that he selected the site and guided the actual construction. In the limited confines of the building is a complex of 21 statues, centering on the primordial Buddha Dainichi Nyorai (Vairocana) and arranged to represent a multidimensional mandala. The effect of the ensemble is overwhelming.

Though the five-story pagoda was not completed until 50 years after Kukai's entry into eternal Samadhi, at the very planning stage, he petitioned the imperial court to have huge trees on Higashiyama mountain felled for use in its building. In the process, trees designated as sacred to the Fushimi Inari Taisha shrine were felled by mistake. Reparations and apologies were made, and Fushimi Inari Taisha became a tutelary Shinto shrine of the Buddhist temple To-ji. Even today, on May 3 of each year, the Inari Kanko-sai festival procession begins with treats provided by Buddhist priests in front of the Keiga-mon gate of To-ji.

Outstanding Achievements

Kukai achieved immortal results as an educator in the capital of his day. In China he had been astonished to see that each town district in the Tang capital Chang'an had its own school. By contrast, a state college was the only school in the Japanese capital Heian-kyo. Only children of aristocrats were admitted; but, upon graduation, they were guaranteed advances in government service. Dissatisfied with the college, Kukai himself dropped out after two years and chose a peripatetic life-style in the mountains and forests.

He described the conditions for a real education as follows: "Study with many outstanding people. Rely on others for food and clothing so that concentration on studies can be total. And live a stable life."

He founded the Shugei Shuchi-in (School of Arts and Sciences), the first privately operated college in Japan, and frequently insisted that it should provide meals for all students. Located in the To-ji compound, it opened in the mansion of Fujiwara Tadamori (785–840) and accepted students regardless of lineage or financial status. The Shugei Shuchi-in was one of Kukai's major achievements in the histories of both Japanese education and school food provision.

Legends about Kukai are found all over Japan—on Kyushu and Shikoku and even in Nagano and Iwate. Restoration of the immense Sanuki Manno Lake (Nakatado County, Kagawa Prefecture), the largest irrigation reservoir in Japan, is attributed to his powers. In accomplishing this work, he applied civil engineering skills learned in Tang-dynasty. He is also said to have applied prayers and austerities as a rainmaker.

Building of the Kodo, from the _Kobo Daishi Gyojo E-kotoba_ picture scrolls, Vol. 9
Paper; width 34 cm, length 1,160 cm (Vol. 9); Namboku-cho period (1336–92); Japanese Important Cultural Property; possession of the To-ji
The scroll depicts the building of the Kodo (Lecture Hall), intended by Kukai to house a group of Buddhist statues creating a multidimensional version of a mandala. The scene depicted gives a good idea of construction work that relied solely on human power.

名宝と文化財
Treasures and Cultural Properties
Original text by Takayuki Yamazaki

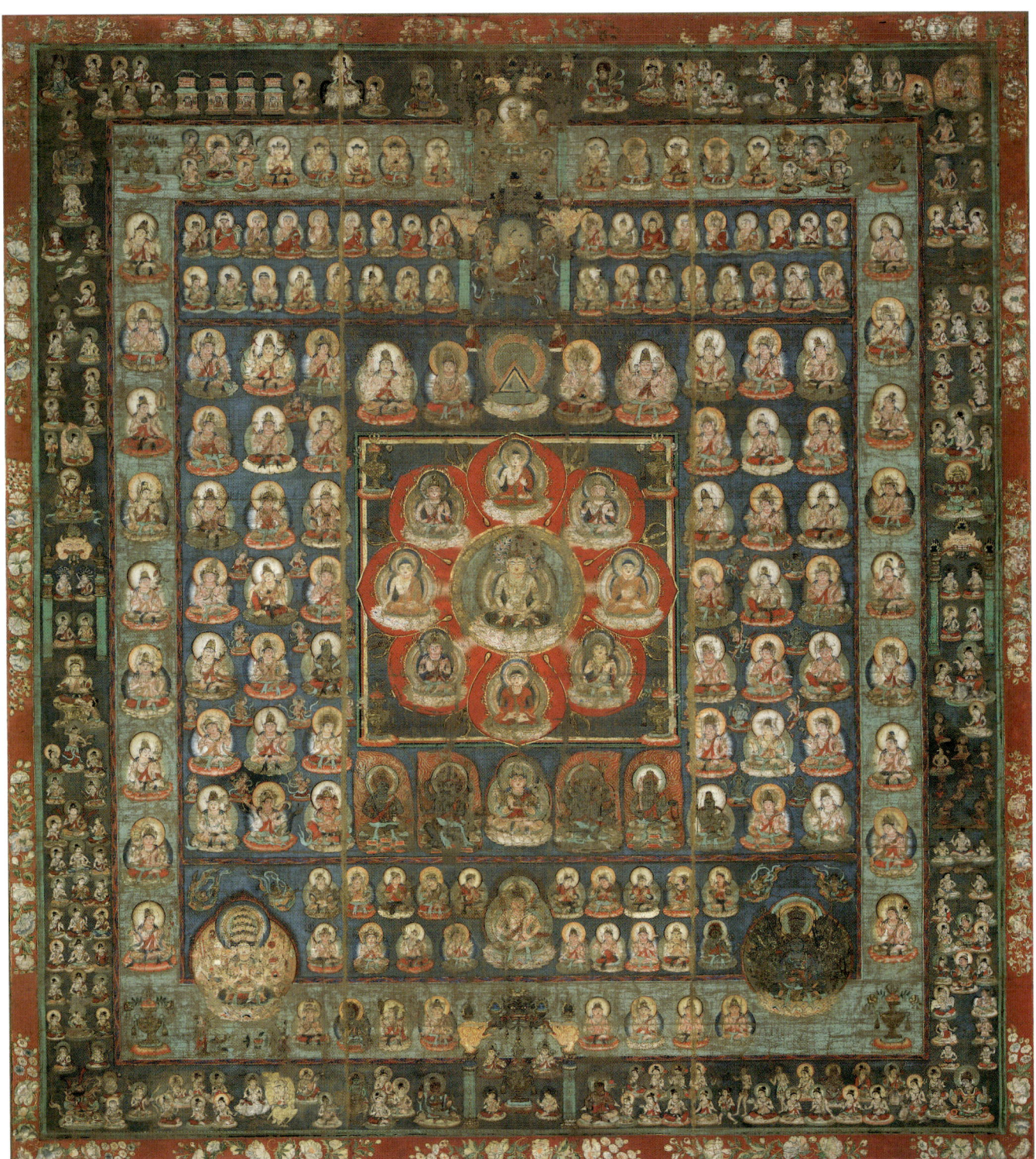

The Womb-world Mandala (Sai-in version)
Silk; vertical dimension 183.6 cm, horizontal dimension 163.0 cm; Heian period (794–1185); Japanese National Treasure
The Womb-world Mandala depicts the fundamental teaching that, as life abides in and emerges from the mother's womb, so everything in the universe emerges from the Buddha Dainichi Nyorai (Vairocana). Positioned in the center in a lotus flower, Dainichi Nyorai is surrounded by other Buddhas, bodhisattvas, and Wisdom Kings. Various divine beings are placed on the outermost border. Like the lotus, which bears seeds in the flower, each human being possesses the bud of the Buddha nature and can unite with Dainichi Nyorai if that bud is brought to flower. Overall, the mandala resembles a beautiful celestial chart.

The Diamond-world Mandala (Sai-in version)
Silk; vertical dimension 183.6 cm, horizontal dimension 164.2 cm; Heian period; Japanese National Treasure
Each of the nine compartments in the mandala contains circles in which are represented Dainichi Nyorai and other Buddhas and bodhisattvas. Whereas the Womb-world Mandala is pictorial in nature, the Diamond-world Mandala is more diagrammatic. From the bottom right square upward and then to the left, it suggests stage-by-stage progression toward the center; that is, toward enlightenment. The individual compartments of the mandala are separated by bands in which are depicted Vajra, or diamond ritual weapons, which represent separation from the earthly life. This accounts for the word "diamond" in its name.

Mandalas: The Essence of Shingon Esoteric Buddhism

Two Mandalas

When traveling to Tang-dynasty (618–907) China as a visiting student in the early ninth century, Kukai came into contact with Esoteric-Buddhist teachings, the newest thing in Buddhism at the time. After studying with and being recognized as orthodox successor by the monk Huiguo, he returned home, taking with him the scriptures, paintings, and ritual articles he would need to spread Esoteric-Buddhist teachings in Japan. The paintings included portraits of Esoteric-Buddhist founders and mandalas. The mandalas were especially prized as means to express the deepest Esoteric philosophies, which are hard to reveal verbally or in scripture.

The Mandalas of the Two Worlds represent the Esoteric-Buddhist cosmos centered on the Buddha Dainichi Nyorai (Vairocana). At the same time, they are the fundamental source of the intense power emitted by Esoteric Buddhism.

Original and Surviving Versions

Operating between the Womb-world Mandala and the Diamond-world Mandala, the ascetic carries out Esoteric-Buddhist practices to effect a union with Dainichi Nyorai. Through this process, called *Sokushin Jobutsu* (attaining Buddhahood in the present body), he or she acquires Dainichi Nyorai's transcendent power, which makes it possible to protect the nation from calamity, pray for good harvests and the healing of illness, and exorcise external enemies.

While in China, Kukai had full-scale (*genzu*) mandalas made. At first intended to be installed at To-ji, they have been lost. But, though partly damaged, copies considered to represent the *genzu* format and made during the Heian (794–1185) and Kamakura (1185–1333) periods survive.

The mandalas transmitted to the Sai-in (the western compound surrounding the Miedo) are somewhat small and reveal differences in drawing pattern. They seem to represent a tradition different from that of the Genzu Mandalas. But these Heian-period mandalas are in a good state of preservation, have a dignified tone, and are the oldest multicolor versions in Japan.

Wisdom Kings—Wrathful Guardians

Characteristics of Esoteric-Buddhist Statuary

The multidimensional mandala in the Kodo (see page 10) consists of 21 statues arranged on a large dais (*shumidan*). In the center of the dais are the Five Dhyani Buddhas (Gochi Nyorai), surrounding the main image Buddha Dainichi Nyorai (Vairocana). To the east of this central group are the Five Great Bodhisattvas (Godai Bosatsu). To the west are the Five Wisdom Kings (Godai Myo-ō), with the Wisdom King Fudo Myo-ō in the center.

The Five Dhyani Buddhas represent the wisdom of Dainichi Nyorai, who controls the whole universe. The Five Great Bodhisattvas employ mercy to explain the Buddhist Law to human beings. Buddha emanations, the Five Wisdom Kings use majestic power to guide human beings. The Five Wisdom Kings are distinctive to Esoteric Buddhism, which was influenced by Hinduism while it evolved in India. Various strange wrathful aspects, including multiple heads and multiple limbs, symbolize their might. Such Indian deities as Shiva too sometimes assume superhuman shapes to terrify people.

Apparently craftsmen who had participated in building the temple Todai-ji, in Nara, were called upon to take part in creating statues for To-ji. Sculpture at the older temple employed a wood-frame core covered with lacquer-soaked layers of hemp cloth and a kind of sawdust paste. The identical method appears in various parts of the To-ji Wisdom King statues, suggesting the work of the same craftsmen. Probably artisans working at To-ji found it difficult to apply this method in completely new kinds of sculpture like those of the Wisdom Kings. Consequently, Kukai's direct guidance in both the planning and molding of the figures must have become indispensable. In other words, the statues in the Kodo reflect both Kukai's philosophy and his aesthetic sense.

Standing statue of Wisdom King Kongo Yasha
Wood; figure height 171.8 cm; Heian period; Japanese National Treasure; housed in the Kodo
The Wisdom King statues employ extremely strange forms to display the beings' might. This one has six arms and three heads with five eyes in the central face. Carving four of those eyes in two tiers must have presented considerable technical difficulty. But the splendid power of the forms is impeccable.

Standing statue of Zochoten, Heavenly King of the South
Wood; figure height 184.2 cm; Heian period (794–1185); Japanese National Treasure; housed in the Kodo
Four Heavenly Kings who guard the cardinal directions are positioned at the corners of the dais in the Kodo. Zochoten guards the south. This work has greater volume, more vigor, and a more wrathful expression than the celebrated Four Heavenly Kings of the earlier Tenpyo era (729–49) at Todai-ji temple. Its combination of such details as a beard and an accurate portrayal of forms suggests the sculptor's great abilities. This and all the statues shown on pages 25 to 28 were produced in 839.

Standing statue of Wisdom King Gozanze

Wood; figure height 173.6 cm; Heian period; Japanese National Treasure; housed in the Kodo

One of the Five Wisdom Kings, Gozanze has eight arms and four faces—three in the front and one in the rear of the head. The weapons in each of the hands represent the Wisdom King's might. The name Gozanze refers to the Three Evils of greed, anger, and folly that this wisdom king can defeat. Gozanze tramples on the Hindu deity Shiva (representing worldly desires) and his wife Uma (representing ignorance).

Statue of Taishakuten seated in half-lotus posture

Wood; figure height 105.4 cm; Heian period; Japanese National Treasure; housed in the Kodo

As a sacred warrior in the heavenly realm, the Hindu deva Indra, known in Japanese as Taishakuten, wears armor. In this distinctively To-ji version, he rides an elephant. Taishakuten is paired with Bonten, the Hindu deva Brahma (page 13), who rides on three geese. Both are Indian in origin.

Seated statue of Wisdom King Fudo Myo-ō
Wood; figure height 173.3 cm; Heian period; Japanese National Treasure; housed in the Kodo

The Five Wisdom Kings are emanations of the Five Dhyani Buddhas; Fudo Myo-ō corresponds to Dainichi Nyorai. With hair hanging to one side, eyes wide open, and face turned slightly to the right, he looks straight ahead. This so-called Daishi Style is based on diagrams Kobo Daishi Kukai brought back from China. Characterized by a mood of calm presence, it is the oldest sculptural version of Fudo Myo-ō.

Mounted statue of Wisdom King Daiitoku
Wood; figure height 100.9 cm; Heian period; Japanese National Treasure; housed in the Kodo

This Wisdom King has three main heads, plus three smaller ones on top. Seated on a water buffalo, he has six arms and six legs and is therefore also called the Six-leg Wisdom King. Possessing the power and virtue to conquer evil, he is used in prayers for victory in war. Though his form is weird, the flowing drapery around his loins is beautiful and his bracelets are gorgeous.

Historically Important Works in the To-ji Treasury Museum

A True Treasure House

The To-ji is truly a treasure house of Esoteric-Buddhist art. The To-ji Treasury Museum contains numerous statues, paintings, and craft items including the two statues shown on this page, page 30 and a standing statue of the Thousand-arm Kannon Bodhisattva that was formerly the main image of the old Jikido (Temple Refectory) and was later repaired after having been burned. Buddhist paintings include the Images of Great Five Wisdom Kings (see page 31), used in the Seven-day New Year Ceremonies for the Protection of the Nation, initiated by Kukai and held in the imperial palace, and the folding screens depicting the Twelve Devas employed in the *kanjo* initiation ritual (see page 30).

Among the craft items are ritual appurtenances and priestly stoles received by Kukai from his master Huiguo and bearing witness to the high level of Tang-dynasty craftsmanship.

Standing statue of Tobatsu Bishamonten
Wood; figure height 189.4 cm; Tang-dynasty (618–907) China; Japanese National Treasure; housed in the To-ji Treasury Museum

This statue was once enshrined in the Rajomon gate (see page 19). Legend has it that Bishamonten (Vaisravana), emerged from the earth in the western part of China (Tou-po, or Tobatsu in Japanese) and repelled foreign invaders. The base on which the statue stands consists of an earth goddess and two demons. Only their upper bodies project above the ground. Bishamonten stands with one foot on each hand of the earth goddess. Unlike those of ordinary statues of the same guardian deity, his clothes partake of Western-Chinese elements. The statue is not entirely of wood: a sandy paste-like substance was used to create forms in various parts. Black spheres have been inserted to create the eyes. This work is valuable as one of the few surviving examples preserving Tang-dynasty techniques.

Standing statue of Bodhisattva Jizo
Wood; figure height 162.4 cm; Heian period; Japanese Important Cultural Property; housed in the To-ji Treasury Museum

Said to have come from Sai-ji, one of the pair of temples that once guarded Heian-kyo (present-day Kyoto), this Jizo has the massiveness and flowing garment folds between the legs that are characteristic of the early Heian period. In older Jizo statues, the right arm is extended, and the hand is in the fearlessness mudra (*semui-in*). Having the right hand hold a priest's staff (*shakujo*) is thought to be a modification of later times.

Image of Wisdom King Fudo Myo-ō (from the Images of Great Five Wisdom Kings)
Silk; vertical dimension 153.0 cm, horizontal dimension 128.8 cm; Heian period (794–1185); Japanese National Treasure

The Images of Great Five Wisdom Kings were used in the Shingon-in at the imperial palace. This picture was re-created after an older To-ji treasure house burned in 1127. It preserves the Daishi Style in that the face is turned slightly to the right. At the same time, it demonstrates trends of a new age, as in the narrowed left eye, or the so-called heaven-and-earth eyes (right eye open, left eye squinting). While angry in aspect, it has a charm and grace suitable to an aristocratic period.

Image of Katen (from the Twelve-deva Screens)
Silk; vertical dimension 130.0 cm, horizontal dimension 42.1 cm; painted by Takuma Shoga in 1191 during the Kamakura period (1185–1333); Japanese National Treasure

The Twelve-deva Screens were used to protect the venue for such ceremonies as *kanjo* initiation, in which connections with the Buddha are established and the Esoteric law is transmitted. The Twelve Devas protect the eight directions plus heaven and earth and the sun and moon. Katen (fire deva) is positioned in the southeast and has an aureole of flames. He resembles an old hermit. With its realistic presentation, this image is important because it established the direction for Buddhist painting of the Kamakura period.

『東宝記』歴史的資料

Tobo-ki: Exceptional Historical Material

● Highly Significant Documents

In addition to being a storehouse of Esoteric-Buddhist art, To-ji is an archive of important historical documents. One of them is the *Tobo-ki* (Records of eastern treasures), official temple records of the greatest importance to an understanding of 600 years of history following the founding of To-ji. Housed in the Kanchi-in, a To-ji sub-temple, they were designated a Japanese National Treasure in 1954.

The full set consists of 12 volumes (drafts appended to eight volumes) written by the priest-scholar Goho (1306–62) and his disciple Genpo (1333–98) from the Namboku-cho period (Northern and Southern Courts; 1336–92) to the Muromachi period (1336–1573). The set is divided into the "Buppo-hen," which records the founding of To-ji; the "Hobo-hen," which explains service ceremonies; and the "Sobo-hen," which deals with clerical organization.

The documentary value of the *Tobo-ki* is very great. Conventional Japanese histories nowhere say that Kobo Daishi Kukai, who was put in charge of the temple, changed its name to Kyo-ō Gokoku-ji in keeping with his intention of making it a fundamental training center for Shingon Esoteric Buddhism. Moreover, the *Tobo-ki* is the oldest document to indicate the purpose behind the founding of To-ji. On the other hand, its attributions are vague and given to laconic remarks like, "As a certain document says…."

Goho, who was from Shimotsuke Province (present-day Tochigi Prefecture)—or according to another explanation, from Tajima Province (present-day Hyogo Prefecture)—was the first chief priest of the Kanchi-in, a To-ji sub-temple. He, Master Raiho (1279–1330) of Mount Koya, and Goho's disciple Genpo were learned monks referred to as the "Three Treasures of the To-ji."

An ancient copy of *The Record of a Pilgrimage to China in Search of the Law* by Ennin (794–864), the third abbot of the Tendai School of Buddhism, too was found at the Kanchi-in in 1883 and was designated a Japanese National Treasure. This is a detailed travel diary by the monks Ennin, who visited China when a great persecution of Buddhism was being conducted by the Daoist Emperor Wuzong (814–46). Ennin barely managed to escape to Japan with his life. Though it was widely read until the Kamakura period (1185–1333), thereafter it was forgotten for centuries. Dr. Edwin O. Reischauer (1910–1990), professor at Harvard University and a specialist in Asian studies—subsequently United States ambassador to Japan—spent 20 years translating Ennin's travel diary into English.

● More Priceless Documents

Another famous set of documents owned by To-ji is *Toji Hyakugo Monjo* (Archives of the To-ji temple contained in one hundred boxes) now the property of the Kyoto Prefectural Library and Archives. Consisting of 27,000 articles on 18,000 sheets, it covers events from the Nara (645–794) to the Edo period (1603–1868). Fearing that the documents would be dispersed, Maeda Tsunanori (1643–1724), fifth daimyo of the Kaga (present-day Ishikawa Prefecture), contributed the 100 handsome paulownia-wood boxes mentioned in the title. Tsunanori was so knowledgeable in Japanese and Chinese writings that he set up a prefect of books within the Maeda clan.

The Kyoto prefecture government obtained the archives in 1967, and in 1997 all of the documents were designated Japanese National Treasures. Currently, Tamotsu Uejima, professor emeritus of Setsunan University, and others are categorizing and interpreting them as material on medieval Japanese history, especially the manorial system,

As this brief outline shows, To-ji is a treasury of valuable historical documents. Over the years, they have sometimes been removed for safety in times of fire to places like Daigo-ji temple, in Kyoto, Fushimi Ward. It is said that today, the temple treasury and other repositories preserve so great a store of documents that no one can say for sure what is likely to be discovered.

Tobo-ki
Namboku-cho to Muromachi period; Japanese National Treasure; possession of the To-ji

The 12 volumes of the *Tobo-ki* are contained in a chest-of-drawers made of paulownia wood. They cover the whole history of the To-ji as indicated by an initial dating to the time when the Emperor Kanmu (737–806) had the national capital moved to Heian-kyo (present-day Kyoto).

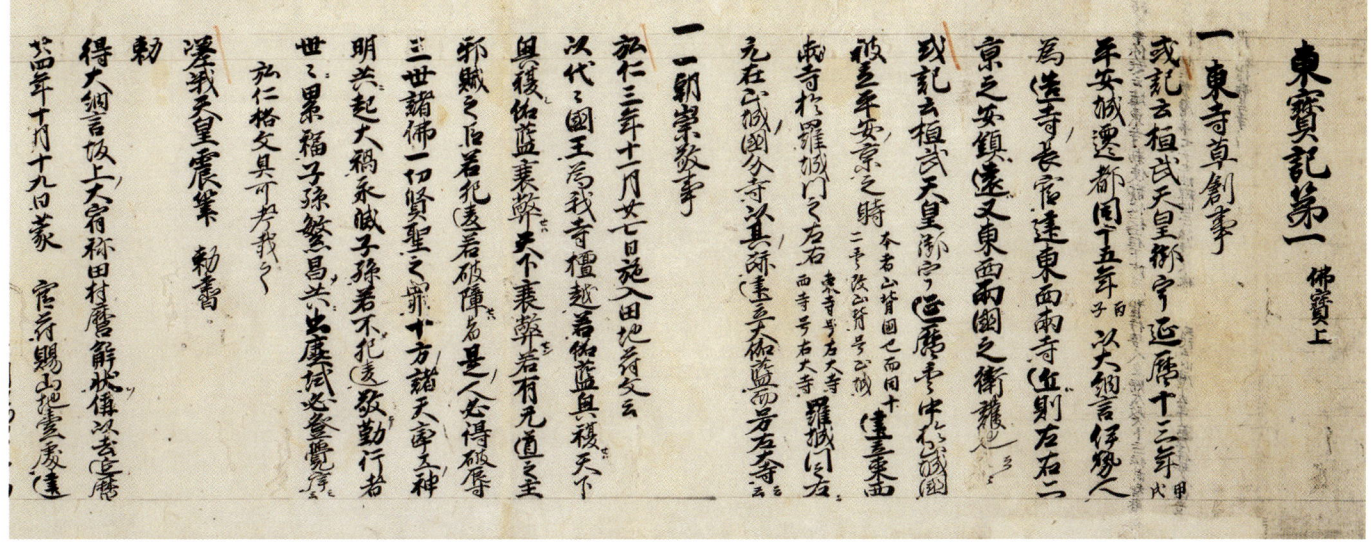

大師筆

弘法大師空海は名筆で知られ、空海が唐から持ち帰って大和(奈良)に伝えたのが、日本での筆づくりの始まりといわれています。
本格的な奈良筆でありながら、ミニサイズでお遍路にも持ち歩ける極細筆「大師筆」は、写経や手紙に欠かせない名品。東寺にて限定販売。
1本入り(墨) 1000円(税込)
2本入り(墨2)、(墨1・赤1) 各1700円(税込) ※いずれも化粧箱入り。

Nighttime illumination of the To-ji Five-story Pagoda in fall

All Photographs ©To-ji 2016
©To-ji (p.34)
©Akira Nakata (p.4, 19)
©Kyoto City Library of Historical Documents (p.18)
©Mizuno Katsuhiko (p.9 bottom)
©Benrido (Cover and other pages)

小学館アーカイヴス
古寺を巡る　東寺　英語版

本書は小学館ウイークリーブック『古寺を巡る3　東寺』(2007年発刊)を再編集し英訳したものです。

発行日　2016年12月27日　初版　第1刷
　　　　2024年 6 月19日　　　　 第2刷
発行所　株式会社小学館
　　　　〒101-8001
　　　　東京都千代田区一ツ橋2-3-1
　　　　編集　03-3230-5563
　　　　販売　03-5281-3555

発行人　斎藤　満
編集人　矢野　文子

英文翻訳・DTP　株式会社インターブックス

印刷所　TOPPAN株式会社
製本所　古宮製本株式会社

造本には十分注意しておりますが、印刷、製本など製造上の不備がございましたら「制作局コールセンター」(フリーダイヤル 0120-336-340)にご連絡ください。
(電話受付は、土・日・祝休日を除く 9:30〜17:30)
本書の無断での複写(コピー)、上演、放送等の二次利用、翻案等は、著作権法上の例外を除き禁じられています。本書の電子データ化などの無断複製は著作権法上の例外を除き禁じられています。代行業者等の第三者による本書の電子的複製も認められておりません。

©SHOGAKUKAN 2016 Printed in Japan
ISBN978-4-09-105443-2